ANGELO'S

BAYONET EXERCISE.

NEW EDITION.

ADJUTANT-GENERAL'S OFFICE, HORSE GUARDS,
JULY 1857.

The Naval & Military Press Ltd

Published by the

The Naval & Military Press

in association with the Royal Armouries

Unit 10 Ridgewood Industrial Park,
Uckfield, East Sussex, TN22 5QE
Tel: +44 (0) 1825 749494
Fax: +44 (0) 1825 765701

MILITARY HISTORY AT YOUR FINGERTIPS
www.naval-military-press.com

ONLINE GENEALOGY RESEARCH
www.military-genealogy.com

ONLINE MILITARY CARTOGRAPHY
www.militarymaproom.com

ROYAL
ARMOURIES

The Library & Archives Department at the
Royal Armouries Museum, Leeds, specialises
in the history and development of armour
and weapons from earliest times to the
present day. Material relating to the
development of artillery and modern
fortifications is held at the Royal
Armouries Museum, Fort Nelson.

For further information contact:
Royal Armouries Museum, Library, Armouries Drive,
Leeds, West Yorkshire LS10 1LT
Royal Armouries, Library, Fort Nelson, Down End Road, Fareham PO17 6AN

Or visit the Museum's website at
www.armouries.org.uk

ANGELO'S

BAYONET EXERCISE.

NEW EDITION.

ADJUTANT-GENERAL'S OFFICE, HORSE GUARDS,
JULY 1857.

𝔓𝔲𝔟𝔩𝔦𝔰𝔥𝔢𝔡 𝔟𝔶 𝔄𝔲𝔱𝔥𝔬𝔯𝔦𝔱𝔶,
BY
JOHN W. PARKER AND SON,
445, WEST STRAND, LONDON.

CONTENTS.

PLATES.

INTRODUCTORY REMARKS.

THE Drill Officers are to understand clearly that, when the Recruits have completed the " Preparatory and Drill Exercises," they need no longer follow the precise order in which they are here given, nor seldom be required to repeat them, but more particularly practised in the " Review Exercise," where each movement is shown, and is to be performed with such celerity, as to give the thrust effectively; and every man should be made so perfect in the movements as to be able to give any thrust separately, or to change quickly from one movement to another, with such variation from the regular order of the drill, as the Instructor may require.

A preparatory explanation of whatever portion of the Exercise the Instructor is about to teach, will tend to make his subsequent instructions more easily understood; and he should exemplify them personally with a musket in his hands, so as to show, by his own position and movements, what he requires the recruit to perform, who should not at first be too rigorously pressed as to exactness, but gradually brought to it by repetition, or further explanation.

Reference also to the Figures which accompany the Instructions will often point out more clearly the positions, &c., than any verbal explanations would effect; and a well-informed Instructor, at the conclusion of the Drill, may show how the instructions just given are applicable either for attack or defence.

The tone of commands should be distinct and to the full extent of the voice; those which serve as a caution should be in clear language, slightly dwelling on the last word; and those for execution in a brief and firm manner.

To attain a good and strong position, the limbs should never be rigid, as the least stiffness retards the promptness of action which is so requisite in giving effect to the bayonet; and the soldier who has confidence in knowing how to make a timely use of it, will not only be more daring when his musket is unloaded, but more cool in his firing; and when placed as a sentry, or acting as a skirmisher, he may often have recourse to his bayonet, and thereby reserve his fire, until absolutely forced to give it.

To deliver the thrust in a proper direction, a cross bar upon poles may be erected, from which balls are suspended, and a squad being drawn up in front, should be practised in giving point at them.

In the Manual and Platoon Exercises there is no instruction for the bayonet, excepting the upright position of "Charge Bayonet," and how to fix or unfix it, and the soldier is there left to make use of it in action any way he pleases; to obviate this deficiency the present Exercise has been formed, so as to give him a knowledge of the advantages to be derived from it, either in the ranks, in the mêlée after a charge, or when acting individually; and the movements are such as can be acquired by men of the most ordinary strength and capacity,—in fact it tends to invigorate the limbs throughout, giving additional force and elasticity to the body, and being performed both with the right and left hand and leg to the front, the soldier gains the proper balance of position—becomes stronger and firmer upon his legs—and the musket itself feels ultimately of less weight in the hand.

So much, indeed, are the arms, legs, and body brought equally into action, that the recruit may commence with the Bayonet Exercise as tending to set him up, by suppling his limbs in a more effective manner than by the usual preparatory exercises to that effect.

BAYONET EXERCISE.

SECTION I.

As soon as the Recruit is sufficiently instructed in "Marching, the Facings, &c., Shoulder Arms, Port Arms, and Charge Bayonet" of the Manual Exercise, Squads (not exceeding sixteen men) may fall in with shouldered arms in single rank, and close files, and be formed in two ranks for Drill Practice, by the following Words of Command.

Prepare for Bayonet Exercise—Right Files stand fast, Left Files go to the Right About.

Quick March—Left Files move four paces to the Rear, halt and front.

Port Arms—As usual.

Charge Bayonet—As usual.

Slow Time—Caution, and being now in the "First Position" of the Exercise, the feet are at right angles, the left pointing to the front, which direction of the feet is to be retained also in the following Positions:

Second Position—Draw back the right foot about twenty-four inches, the body resting upon it, the heels in line with each other, both knees bent, and kept well apart, the right directly over the foot, the left easy and flexible, pointing to the front.

Third Position—Advance the body by the extension of the right leg, and the bending forward of the left leg, without moving or raising the feet.

Second Position—As before.

Advance—Move forward the left foot about six inches, and follow with the right, the same length of step.

Retire—Step back with the right foot about six inches, replacing the left as before.

Double Advance—Straightening the knees bring up the right foot to the " First Position," and with the left, step out to the " Second Position."

Double Retire—Move back the left foot to the " First Position," and with the right, fall back to the " Second Position."

First Position—Straightening the knees, bring up the right heel to the left.

Shoulder Arms—As usual, resuming the proper front.

Order Arms—As usual.

Stand at Ease—As usual.

In the above and following Drill, each movement may be repeated according to the judgment of the Drill Officer, and to the capacity and strength of the Recruit, but they must not be kept too long in any movement; and where it is necessary for one, or more, to repeat any particular part or portion of the Drill, the rest should remain "Standing at Ease."

SECTION II.

After coming to "Attention," "Shoulder Arms," "Port Arms," and "Charge Bayonet," (as before) the Drill is resumed by

Drill Practice—Caution.

Guard—Fall back to the "Second Position," with the knees well apart, the back and neck bent and chest drawn in, the musket retaining the position of "Charge Bayonet," except that by keeping its original elevation from the ground, the right wrist should now be upon the upper part of the hip, and the left elbow close to, and in front of the body, with the thumbs round, and grasping the stock and barrel of the musket, the point of the bayonet directed towards the height of a man's breast. *Vide* Plate I.

PLATE I.—GUARD.

Balance Arms—Relax the fingers of both hands, so that the musket rests entirely without motion, and balanced on the palm of the left hand.

As you were—Resume the hold of the musket.

Slow Time—Caution.

Point—Gradually and slowly advance the musket to the front, the height of a man's breast, as far as the arms and extension by the "Third Position" can reach, with the right elbow rather under and close to it, and without quitting the hold, or losing the balance, (which must be attended to in all thrusts,) and the head lowered in taking aim, as when required at the "Present," previous to firing. *Vide* Plate II., p. 15.

Two—Resume slowly the position of "Guard."

Low—Turn the musket, the sling being uppermost, and raise the butt and elbow, as high as the head, the back of the hand towards the right ear, and bayonet pointing downwards to the front. *Vide* Plate III.

PLATE III.—LOW.

PLATE II.—POINT.

Point—As before, but downwards, and as it gradually descends, turn the barrel upwards—in which position it finally is, on the delivery of every thrust. *Vide* Plate IV.

PLATE IV.—POINT.

Two—Resume the position of "Low."

High—Turn the barrel upwards and raise the bayonet above, and in front of the head, by lowering the right wrist to the hip. *Vide* Plate V.

PLATE V.——HIGH.

Point—As before, but upwards.   *Vide* Plate **VI**.

PLATE VI.—POINT.

Two—Resume the position of "High."

Shorten Arms—Lower the point of the bayonet direct to the front, and carry back the butt of the musket to the full extent of the right arm, the barrel resting upon the thick part of the left arm, and the left leg extended. *Vide* Plate VII.

PLATE VII.—SHORTEN ARMS.

Point—As before, direct to the front, as in Plate II.

Two—Resume the position of "Shorten Arms."

Second Point—Prepare as for "High," except that the point of the bayonet is now direct upwards. *Vide* Plate VIII.

PLATE VIII.——SECOND POINT.

Point—Raise the musket to the full extent of the right arm, and lower the left along the thigh, with both legs extended. *Vide* Plate IX.

PLATE IX.—POINT.

Two—Resume the Position of "Second Point."

Guard—As before

Shoulder Arms—As usual.

Order Arms—As usual.

Stand at Ease—As usual.

In *repeating* the thrusts of the above practice, the command " As you were" may be given, instead of " Two."

The generality of men, and particularly those unin-structed, will thrust or strike with the musquet, retaining the hold of it by both hands; whereas the man instructed to point with *one* hand only (as above) will be able to keep his opponent at such a distance, as to have con-siderable advantage over him ; and in making this " Point" (to the front) the body must bend forward, without restraint or stiffness, being well supported on the haunches.   In general the point reaches nine feet when acting individually, and eight feet in close files.

It must, however, be borne in mind that—except in thrusting " High" as in " Second Point," where the left hand can more readily resume the grasp of the musket—great caution and care must be used, when so delivering a thrust direct to the front, as the assailant is likely to be disarmed, or his musket so thrown out of the line of de-fence, as not to be easily recovered; in fact, such a thrust should only be resorted to, when there is every chance of its being given effectively, and having the left hand quite prepared to resume its hold.

SECTION III.

On resuming the Drill as pointed out in the previous Section, it proceeds with—

Guard—As before.

Variations of the Point—Caution.

Right—The feet remaining steady, turn the body to the right front, and present the bayonet in that direction.

Left—The body and bayonet turned to the left front.

Low—As before, but in the direction of the left front.

High—As before, but still as in the preceding direction.

Right—Turn the body and bayonet to the right front. still keeping in the position of " High."

Low—As before, but in the direction of the right. front.

Guard—As before.

The above variations are to be repeated, and the " Point" given, as before, slowly, from each position ; and the Drill Practice is also to be gone through in close files, the squad being reformed in single rank for that purpose.

The movements of this, and of the preceding section, are then to be practised in a quicker time, the *latter* part of the thrust being given the quickest, and in withdrawing the musket the *first* part should be *so* performed.   This will be a preparation for the " Review Exercise."

SECTION IV.

In order to bring the body and limbs into equal action on both sides, the preceding practices should be performed with the right shoulder and foot to the front, for which purpose the squad, being brought to the position of " Guard," the command is given.

About—Straighten the knees, and raise the musket nearly to the " Recover Arms," at the same time turning upon the heels so that the right foot points to the rear, the left foot to its left ; and smartly changing the hold of the musket, with the right hand for the " Balance," and the left grasping the small of the stock, sink down again to the position of " Guard," by bending the knees, and having the weight of the body now transferred to the left leg.

The whole of the preceding Practices are then to be gone through by the same words of command, and the squad is brought to its proper front from the position of " Guard " as follows.

About—As before directed.

Shoulder Arms—As usual.

Order Arms—As usual.

Stand at Ease—As usual.

This is a very essential portion of the Exercise, by giving equal practice to both arms and legs, in fact strengthening every part of the body ; and the Instructor may have some idea of the proper position by holding up to the light the pages on which the figures are delineated, and so (on the reverse page) be able sufficiently to distinguish the figure with the *right* foot in advance, and the musket to the *left* of the body.

SECTION V.

REVIEW EXERCISE.

The word of command "Two" is no longer required for the second motion, as the "Point" is given at once, and the musket drawn back to the position from which it was delivered, and in quick, but marked, time.

The Company or Battalion being in Line at "Shoulder Arms," and closed ranks, the command is given,

Prepare for Bayonet Exercise—The Right Files of the Front Rank stand fast; the remainder of both ranks go to the "Right About."

Quick March—The Files which have faced about move direct to the Rear; the Left Files of the Front Rank, four paces; the Right Files of the Rear Rank, seven paces; the Left Files of the Rear Rank, eleven paces; each man halting and fronting at his proper distance, and the Ranks dressing by the Right.

Review Exercise—Caution.

Guard—As before.

Point—Delivered to the Front and returning to "Guard," but there should be a pause to mark the time when each "Point" is delivered, before returning to the position from which it is given, each movement being swiftly and smartly executed by the following words of command, in succession, viz.—*Low—Point—High— Point—Shorten Arms—Point—Second Point—Point— Guard—Right—Point—Left—Point—Low—Point— High—Point—Right—Point—Low—Point—Guard —Shoulder Arms—Order Arms—Stand at Ease.*

The above movements are then to be gone through with the right shoulder and leg forward, the command "*About*" being given from the position of "Guard;" by following the instructions as laid down in the preceding Section, and on the Exercise being finished, the Company or Battalion (after coming to the "Shoulder Arms") is reformed "Two Deep," by the command,

Form Line—Quick March—The three Rear Ranks move up to their proper places, and the whole is brought to "Stand at Ease" as hitherto directed.

The Exercise should be practised (and shown also, if required, at an Inspection) in Two Ranks, by the Left Files of each Rank moving up to the Left of their respective Right Files, by the words of command, *Form Ranks —Quick March*; the Two Ranks are, consequently, at eight paces distant, and the Right or Left Files being brought "About," (thereby giving practice in the Drill to both,) the movements may be performed to the Front and to the Rear at the same time.

When the men are quite perfect in the Exercise, it may be performed without any further words of command than *Perform Bayonet Exercise*, upon which they commence, as usual, with "Guard," going regularly through, and executing the movements smartly, but marking the time between each, according to the ordinary time in marching.

SECTION VI.

ATTACK AND DEFENCE AGAINST THE SWORD.

The preceding directions are the movements for the
" Bayonet Exercise," which becomes an addition to
the regular " Manual and Platoon Exercise;" but for
action individually, where such occurrence takes place—
a knowledge of " Time " and " Measure " is desirable,
and may be attained by the following Practice against
men, armed with *practice* swords, and the bayonets
prepared in the same way as *foiled* lances; or where these
cannot be obtained, the Practice may be carried on with
muskets and the sword-practice sticks, in lieu of the
bayonets and swords; in which case the ranks must be a
full half-pace nearer to each other.

For this purpose a Squad (in two ranks) is formed
and extended, so that the files are two paces apart, with
an interval of three paces between the ranks—the front
rank having the swords.

The Front Rank being at " Slope Swords," and the
Rear Rank at " Shoulder Arms " the command is given.

Words of Command.	*Front Rank.*	*Rear Rank.*
Front Rank— *Right About* *Face*	As usual.	
Guard.	Come to the " Outside Guard " in " Second Position."	Come to " Guard."

Words of Command. *Front Rank.*		*Rear Rank.*
Prove Distance.		Point slowly so as to touch slightly the breast of the opponent.
Two.		Resume the "Guard."
Point.	Defend by the "First Guard," retaining the " Second Position," in which remain (throughout the Practice) until " Slope Swords."	Thrust at the upper part of the breast, and return to " Guard," the same being done in the following "Points"
Point.	" Second Guard."	Thrust, &c.
Point.	"Third Guard," low, with an extended arm.	Thrust at the body below the arm.
Point.	" Fourth Guard," in the same way as above.	Thrust, as above.
Point.	" Fifth Guard."	Thrust at the breast.
Point.	"Sixth Guard," and prepare to " Parry."	Thrust, &c.
Point.	" Parry," as usual.	Thrust, &c.
Shoulder Arms—Come to the "Slope Swords."		Come to the "Shoulder Arms."

For " Drill Practice," each movement is to be divided into three motions; the first for the attack; the second for the defence; the third for returning to "Guard" with the bayonet: *viz.*, (by word of command) *One*—Point (bayonet); *Two*—defensive Guard (sword); *Three*—returning to " Guard " (bayonet).

The same Drill should be formed in two motions; the first being the first and second (as above) combined into one motion, the second being the above third motion.

This Practice shows that the first six " Guards" and " Parry" of the " Sword Exercise," defend against the thrust of the bayonet, the " Fifth Guard" being the most effective, as it enables the swordsman to seize the musket with his left hand, and deliver the cut " Six " at his opponent's neck; this, however, (and other similar attempts,) is counteracted by quickly coming to the " Shorten Arms," and instantly striking with the " Point," *vide* Plates X., XI., XII., the practice, being made a continuation of the " Attack and Defence " between the two weapons, as follows, but first in two Motions.

Words of Command.	*Front Rank.*	*Rear Rank.*
Guard.	Come to " Outside Guard," rather inclining to " Fourth Guard"	Come to " Guard."
Point.	Defend by " Fifth Guard," and raise the Left Hand ready to seize the musket. *Vide* Plate X., p. 30.	Thrust at the breast and remain as in Drill Practice.

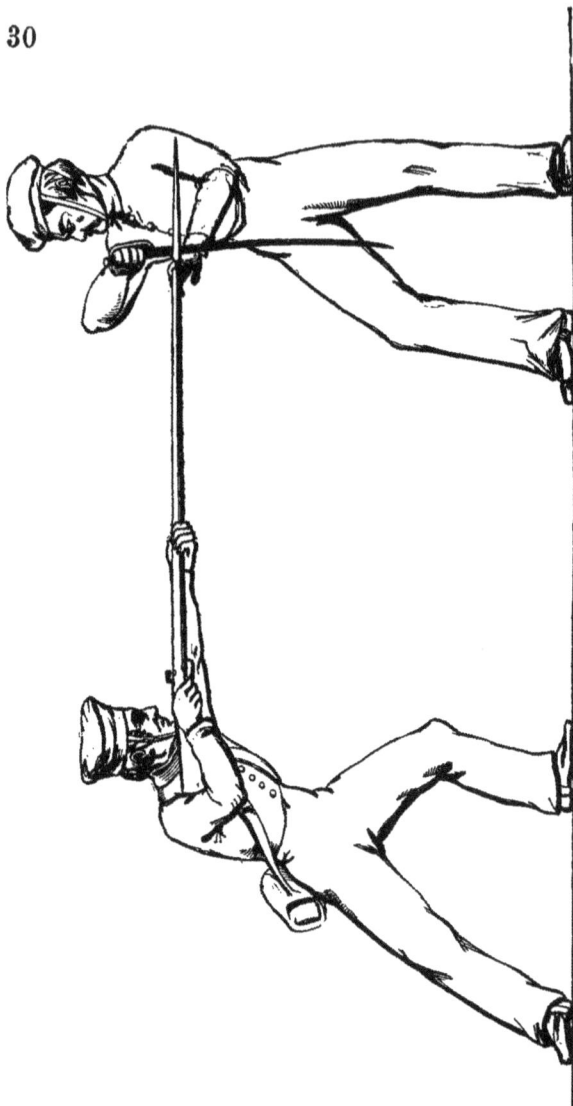

PLATE X.—ATTACK AND DEFENCE.

Words of Command.	Front Rank.	Rear Rank.
Two.	Seize the barrel of the musket and force it down to the left, bringing forward the Left Leg, and prepare for Cut "Six." *Vide* Plate XI.	Remain in the previous position, with the bayonet forced downwards.

PLATE XI.—ATTACK AND DEFENCE.

Words of Command.	*Front Rank.*	*Rear Rank.*
Guard.	" Outside Guard," as before, and returning to " Second Position."	" Guard," as before.
Point.	Defend, as before, and seize the musket, advancing the left leg. Refer to Plate XI.	Thrust, as before.
Guard.	" Outside Guard," as before.	" Guard," as before.
Point.	Defend, and move forward, as before, to seize the musket. *Vide* Plate XII. p. 33.	Thrust, as before, and " Shorten Arms" as quickly as possible, to prevent the musket being seized.
Guard.	" Outside Guard," as before.	" Guard" as before.
Shoulder Arms.	Come to " Slope Swords."	Come to " Shoulder Arms."

The Swordsman may return a Thrust from each Guard—from the " First" and " Third," the " Second Point"—from the " Second" and " Fifth," the " First Point"—from the " Fourth," " Sixth," and " Parry," the " Third Point"—also the Cut " Six" from " First" and " Fifth" Guards—the Cut " Five" from " Second" and " Sixth" Guards—the Cut " Three" from " Fourth Guard;" and the Cut " Four" from " Third" Guard.

Although the above applies more particularly to the " Sword Exercise" it is good practice both for the Swordsman and Bayonetteer—the latter coming to the " Shorten

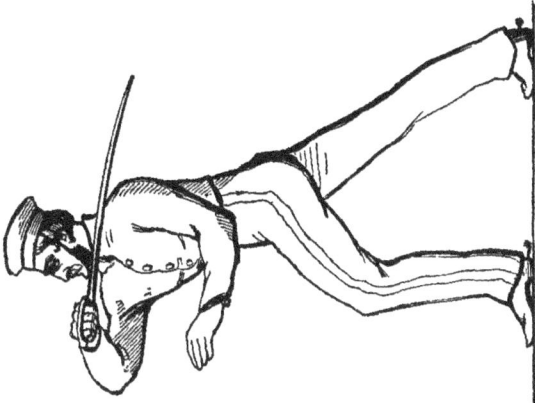

PLATE XII.—ATTACK AND DEFENCE.

Arms," and quickly pointing in return. The Swordsman should recollect that all defences to the left, or "Inside Guards" are more effective than those on the right, or "Outside Guards," from the bayonet then having less power of resistance, although in all, except the "Fifth Guard," the bayonet can easily regain its cover of the opponent's body, by yielding sufficiently from the Upper Guards, as instantly to cover the body below the arm, or *vice versa*, from the Lower Guards.

The regular "Guard" covers the opponent's breast with the point of the bayonet, but great caution is requisite to prevent his striking it down, in which case, lowering it is the best, as a very slight pressure of the right hand will raise it ready to thrust, and for those who are good judges of measure, or distance, it is an easier position to engage.

The action of changing from right to left, or *vice versa*, when the point is "High" or "Low," will defend against any thrust similar to the four "Guards" of the Sword Exercise.

GENERAL OBSERVATIONS.

EXPERIENCE has shown how much the "Sword Exercise" improves the Cavalry Soldier in the use of his limbs, whilst the "Manual Exercise" with the musket has rather a tendency to the contrary in the Infantry Soldier; but by the addition of the instructions for the bayonet, every limb is brought into play, and by developing the physical powers of the soldier, whilst gradually inculcating a knowledge of his duty in the field, he becomes a more formidable opponent to the enemy when instructed how to use the bayonet to advantage, as he will then attack with far more confidence, or rely upon it for defence by a species of counter-attack; in fact many men have been cut down by the Cavalry, who probably would have been successful assailants, had they known to what extent the bayonet could have been used, by previous instruction to that effect.

Although the solidity of a compact body of men, is the primary and essential point in a charge, yet a mêlée invariably follows, where any resistance is made; and then which man has the advantage?—the man who knows how to use his weapon with effect, and actually does use the bayonet with its deadly point,—or the other, who either loses, or throws his bayonet away, so as to strike more readily with the butt-end of the musket? In the latter case the failure of a blow exposes him to the opposing bayonet or sword, before he has time to return to any defensive position, whilst in the former, the well-instructed soldier—Cavalry or Infantry—whether with sword, or musket and bayonet, will give two cuts, or thrusts, and more effectively, while the untrained opponent may probably be unable to give either the one or the other.

In the attack a Feint may be used, so as to make an opponent lay himself open to it, by menacing one part, whilst the intention is to direct it at another, and the thrust should be given, as the opponent answers to the feint; or by beating the ground suddenly with the advanced foot, and instantly thrusting wherever the opening offers; or by stepping back quickly, and as the opponent advances, making an instantaneous attack upon him; and either in attack, or defence, advantage may be gained by springing on both legs to the front, or to the rear, or on either side; but much must depend upon individuals accustoming themselves to such practices.

When attacked by more than one opponent, the soldier should endeavour to keep them in his front, either by constantly shifting his position, or availing himself of a wall, or any where so as to prevent their getting· at him by the rear.

The " Second Point" applies to acting against an opponent on ground above, or so placed as that he cannot otherwise be reached.

Against a Horseman, the defence rests mainly upon a counter-attack, by springing aside, so as to avoid the direct motions of the horse, and thrusting at the horseman even at the moment he attempts to point or cut, as the length of the musket and bayonet has an advantage over the sword, and invariably endeavouring to keep on his left side, where he has less power of defending himself or his horse, and cannot reach so far in attacking, as on his right; and every opportunity should be taken of maiming the horse also, by thrusting at his head or flanks, or striking at his hocks as he passes, thereby making him so unruly as to place the rider at the mercy of his opponent.

Against a Lancer, the right side should be gained, and much more caution observed than in a simultaneous cut or thrust of the sword—the lance having nearly an equality in length—but, when singly engaged, the man on foot can more readily preserve the proper distance than he who has to regulate the motions of his horse to attain it.

The practice of the " Sword" against the "Bayonet Exercise" will be equally beneficial to both parties where Squads are formed for that purpose, as it tends to make the Swordsman more effective and gives the Bayonetteer the practice of properly recovering the musket from each thrust without deranging his position, or losing his balance; and as long as he preserves his proper distance, he will have the advantage of keeping out of the opponent's reach, at the same time retaining him within his own, by wielding the longer weapon.

The above Exercise is by no means intended for a system of " Bayonet Fencing," such as is occasionally practised by foreign troops, but it has been formed as more especially adapted to the qualities of the British soldier, giving him sufficient knowledge how to use his bayonet effectively, whenever he is likely to require it; at the same time that it lays the foundation, for those who desire it, to make themselves expert Bayonetteers under all circumstances: in such cases—for loose or independent practice and to prevent injury to the parties engaged,—a ramrod, with a spring attached to it,

may be inserted in the barrel of the musket, so
as to leave the length of a bayonet outside, with
some gutta percha round the top, like the button
of a foil—the practice sticks being used in lieu
of the sword—and on no account whatever without
the masks.

HENRY ANGELO,

Superintendent of Sword Exercise.

www.ingramcontent.com/pod-product-compliance
Lightning Source LLC
Chambersburg PA
CBHW020953030426
42339CB00004B/77